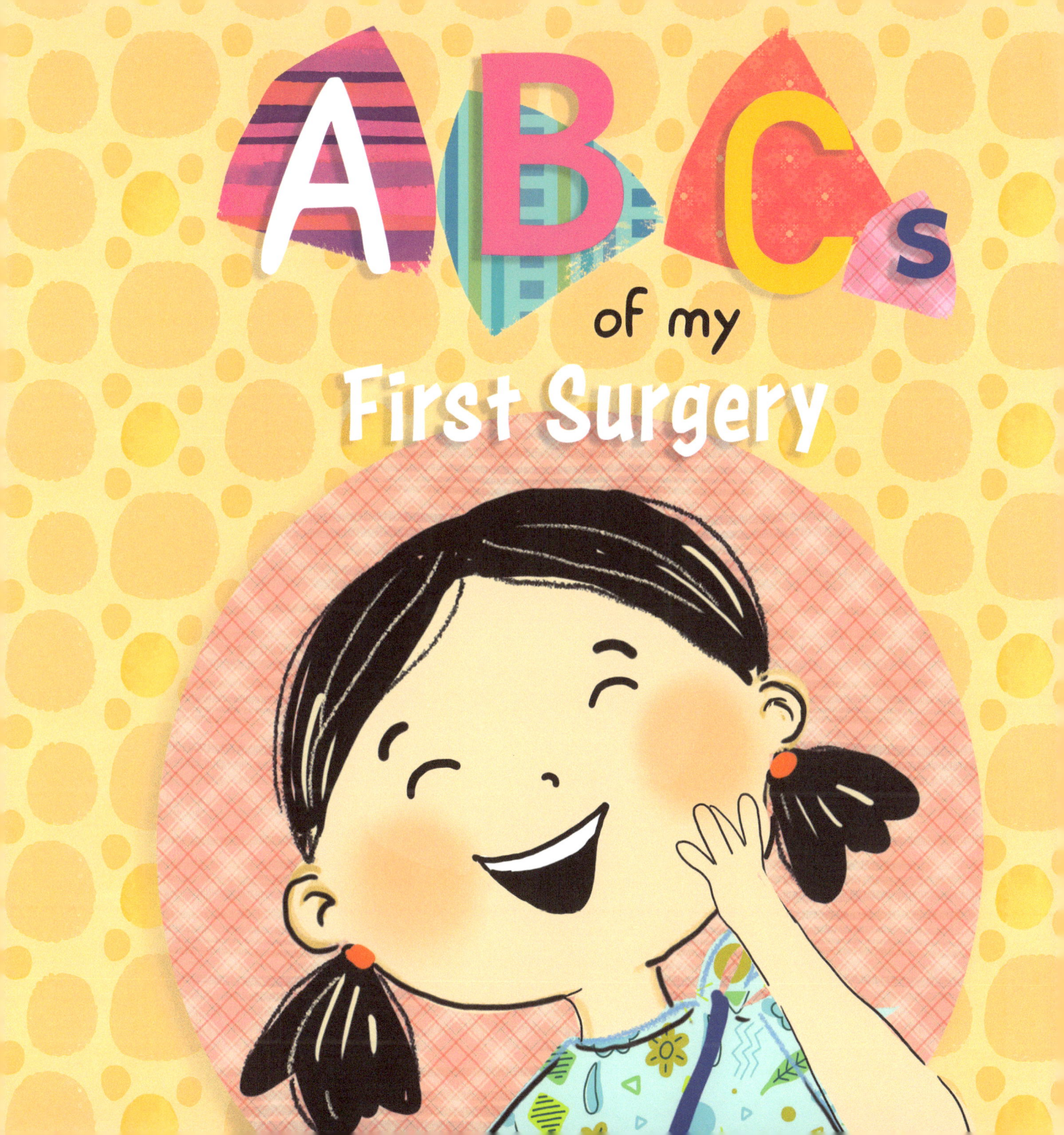

Copyright@2024 F.A. Khan
All rights reserved. No parts of this book are permitted for reproduction or transmission in any form without written permission of the author.
To request permission, contact author at fakhanauthor@gmail.com

Please consult your surgeon and anesthesiologist for any questions relating to health care or preparation for surgery for your child. Each child is unique. The contents of this book are a general representation, not specific to any case.

Library of Congress Number: 2022916219

ISBN:
Ebook – 979-8-9868884-2-2
Paperback- 979-8-9868884-0-8
Hardcover – 979-8-9868884-1-5

Illustrations and Cover Art by Bazma Ahmad
Edited by Robin Katz

Printed in the USA

Dedicated to my family;

    you are the wind beneath my wings.

Hi, I am Maya! I will be having surgery today to fix the broken bone in my arm.

My nurse got me ready for surgery by explaining how the doctors and the whole surgery team will be helping me today. Do you want to know what I learned?

Let's go!

Fun fact: Surgery is done in an operating room in the hospital. That's one reason why it's also called 'having an operation.'

Aa Antibiotics

I will get medicines called **antibiotics**. They knock out infections, which helps keep me healthy. They also make sure I don't develop any new infections while my body heals after surgery.

Bb Blood

The heart is like the body's engine, and blood is the gas that makes my body run. Blood pumps through my heart and then to the other parts of my body to keep me alive. During my surgery, the anesthesiologist will watch my blood pressure to make sure my heart is working well.

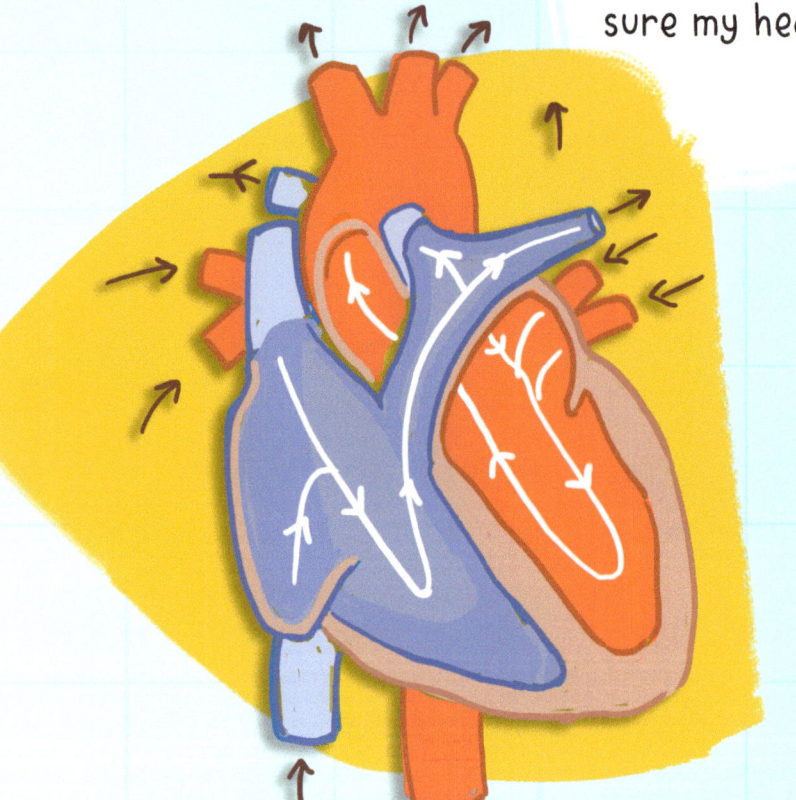

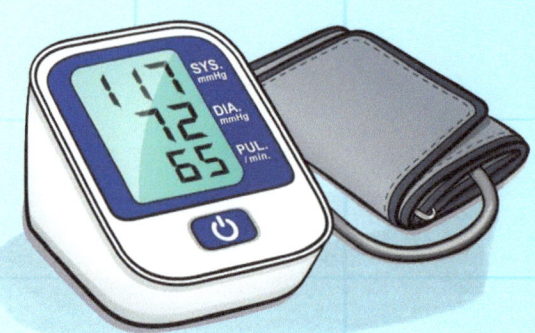

Fun fact: BP (Blood Pressure) is written as two numbers (like a fraction). The top number is the Systolic BP and the bottom number is the Diastolic BP. These tell you how hard your blood is pushing against the walls of the arteries. Normal BP for a five-year-old child falls between 93/55 and 110/70.

Cc Checkup

Before surgery, I needed a Checkup with my Anesthesiologist, Dr. King. She will help put me to sleep for my surgery.

"Maya, while you're asleep, I'll make sure you stay safe and healthy. When you wake up, your broken bones will be fixed. After that, you'll need to rest and heal to be ready to play again!"

Fun fact: During my checkup, she listened to my heart and lungs, she looked into my mouth and examined me from head to toe! I got an A+ !

Dd Doctor

I have a great team of doctors taking care of me. The anesthesiologist will put me to sleep and watch over me. An orthopedic surgeon specializes in fixing broken bones. A pediatrician is a doctor taking care of children. Together, they make sure I will have a safe and successful surgery.

Fun Fact: The surgical team is made up of many other important people including a scrub technician responsible for the items needed to fix my bones, an X-ray technician who shows X-rays taken during surgery, and an OR crew who helps clean and prepare the operating room.

Do you know what an EKG is? It's short for electrocardiogram. A small EKG machine produces a picture of my heart beat's rhythm. If you listen to the heart beat, it sounds like lub-dub, lub-dub. The EKG can seem like a piece of art!

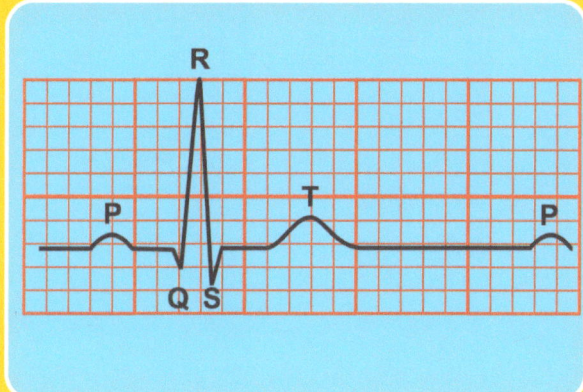

See how the QRS letters resemble castle peaks.

Fun fact: Our hearts have four chambers and four valves. The valves act like doors that open and close and allow blood to move through the heart. Heart sounds are made when these valves open and close.

Fracture

A fracture is a break in a bone. I have badly fractured (broken) my Radius, one of the two bones in my forearm.

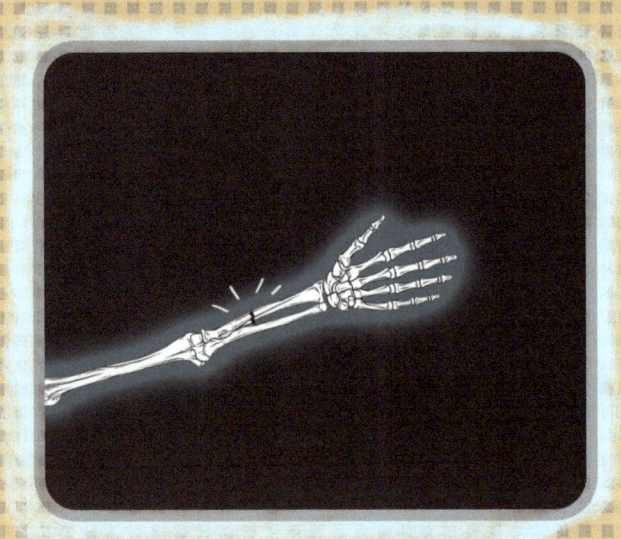

Fun fact: our upper arm bone is called the humerus, and your forearm bones are called the radius and the ulna. Your hand has eight carpal bones, and each finger has bones called phalanges.

G g Gloves

Gloves help keep germs away. All the hospital workers must wash their hands before touching me and wear gloves to protect me.

Fun Fact: Handwashing can prevent many infections, including respiratory and hospital-acquired infections, as well as diarrhea. Always wash your hands like the hospital team members do.

Hospital

Here is the hospital where I have came for my surgery. Many patients stay at hospitals for surgery, special testing, and specialized medical care.

Instruments

The surgeon will use specially designed surgical *instruments* to fix my bones.

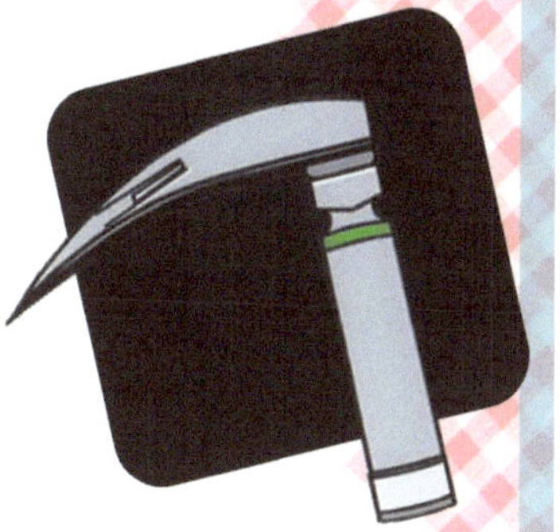

Laryngoscope

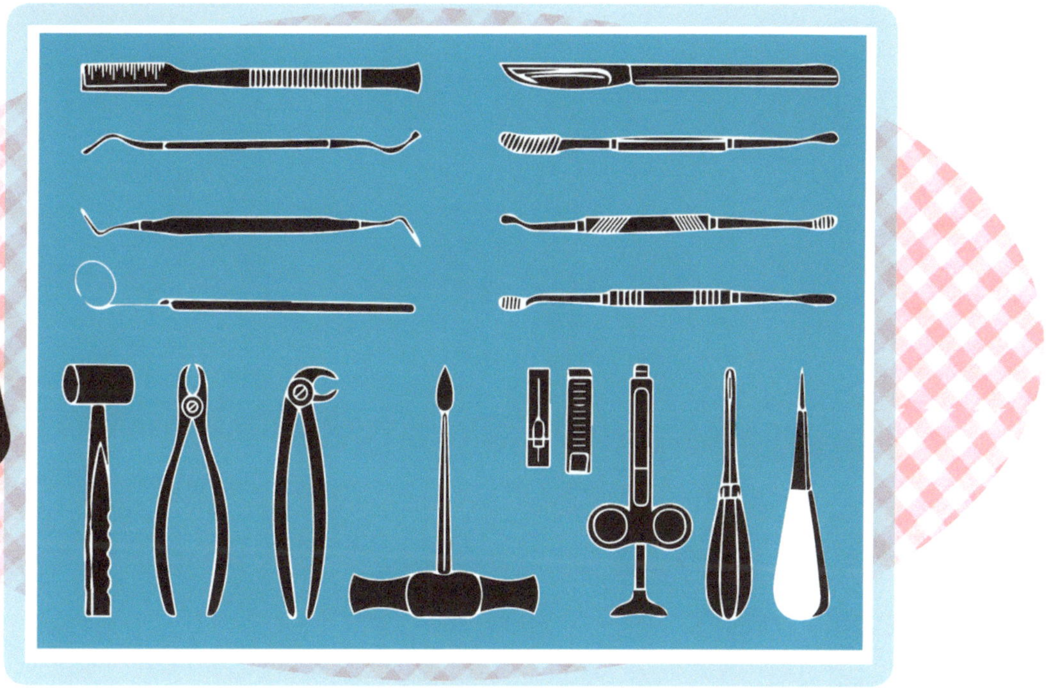

Fun fact: Specialized instruments are used during every kind of surgery. Some of them are scissors for cutting, retractors and forceps for pulling, and special screws for attaching broken bone pieces together. A **Laryngoscope** is another magic instrument for my doctor. It is used to shine a light in my mouth so that they can see where to place the breathing tube.

Jello and Juice

Did you know they'll bring me Jello and juice after my surgery? That's great because I'll probably be thirsty . . . and maybe a bit hungry, too!

Fun fact: NPO (which stands for Nil Per Oral) means not eating or drinking anything before surgery. Not eating or drinking keeps your stomach empty and lets it rest so your body is ready for surgery.

There are so many things in medicine and surgery that start with the letter K ! I'm still learning new things every day. How many do you know? See if you can match the following

1. knee
2. kidney
3. kyphosis
4. ketamine
5. K^+ - potassium
6. keloid
7. keratin
8. karyotype
9. keratitis

1. medicine
2. spine
3. eyes
4. DNA
5. scar
6. protein
7. urine
8. electrolyte
9. joint

Fun fact: Medicines used in anesthesia make you go to sleep by altering neurotransmission at multiple sites of the brain. They also act by reducing pain and anxiety.

Latex

Latex is used to make many of the products you see in medicine, such as gloves, catheters and bandages. My doctor asked about Latex allergy so that they would know whether it was safe for me or not and write it on my allergy band.

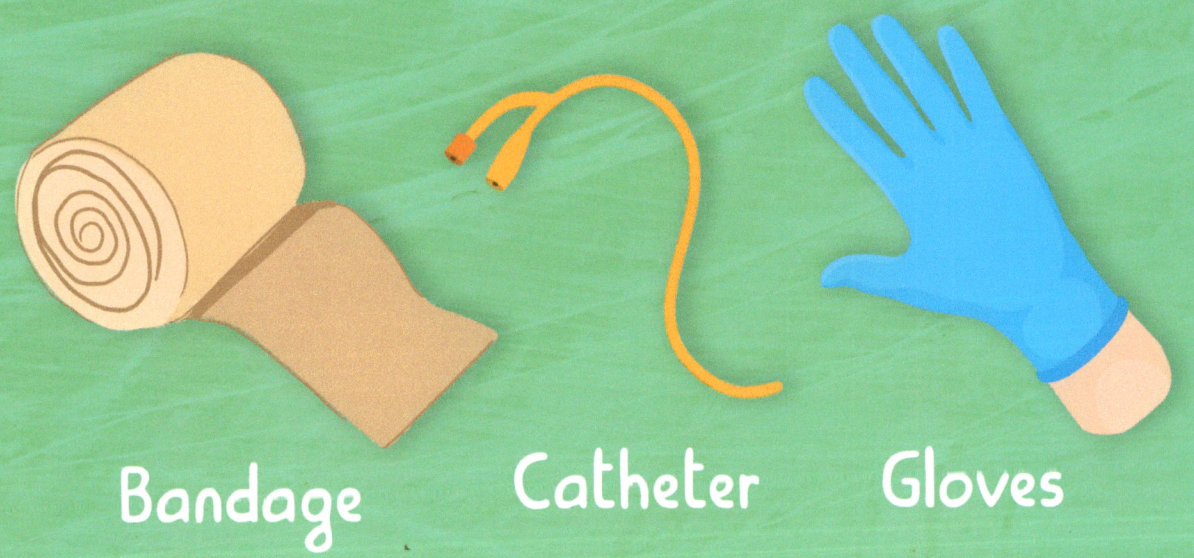

Bandage   Catheter   Gloves

Fun fact: Latex is a protein found in the sap of a rubber tree grown in Africa and Southeast Asia.

 Mask

I get to choose a breathing mask with the special 'sleepy magic gas' that will help me sleep for the surgery. Guess which one is my favorite flavor? STRAWBERRY, GRAPE, BUBBLEGUM.

Fun fact: Nitrous oxide is also known as laughing gas and is used in medical and dental procedures as a sedative. It helps calm anxiety and allows the patient to relax.

Nurse

Kylie is my nurse today. Nurses are very important people. They help take care of you when you are in the hospital. Nurse Kylie will also call my mom during surgery and let her know I'm doing great!

Operating Room

Here is the operating room. This is where incredible things happen! Surgical instruments are expertly handled, and soft music soars while the surgeon fixes my broken bones.

Fun fact: You can listen to music while you are going to sleep. What music would you choose to listen to? I'm going to hear my favorite song, 'Let It Go,' from the movie, 'Frozen.'

Pulse

I learned a cool trick today! I can check my own pulse by feeling my heartbeat when I press on my wrist! Feel this here: As my heart beats, I can feel it here on my wrist near the palm of my hand. The beat I feel in my wrist matches the rhythm of my heart.

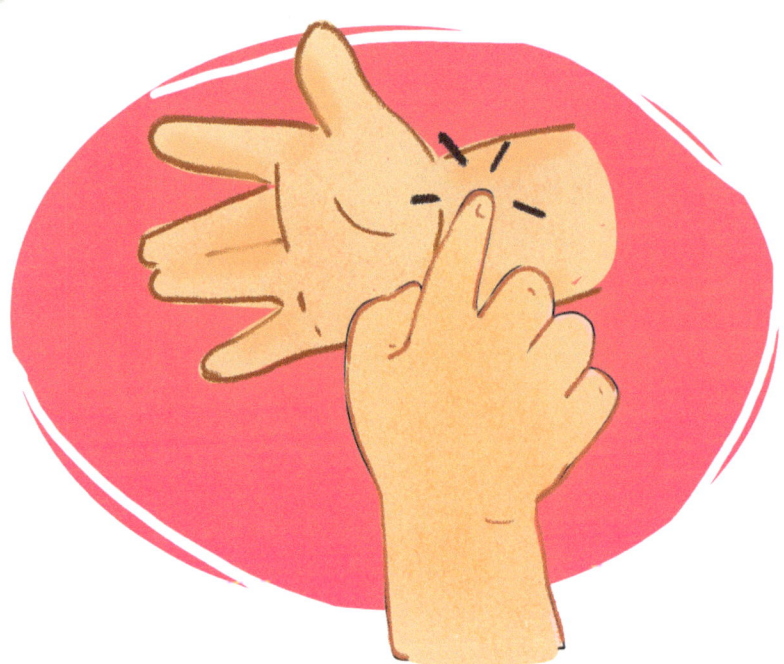

Fun fact: Did you know your heart beats between 60 – 100 times per minute? Feel your pulse today and count how many times your heart is beating in one minute.

Questions

I asked my doctor so many questions! Let me share what I learnt with you.

Question list:

- What is anesthesia?
Medicine that puts you to sleep for surgery

- What is a broken bone called?
A fracture

- When will I eat after surgery?
After you wake up and feel ready to eat, choose light foods that are easy on the stomach.

- Will it hurt? How will you take care of my pain?
It won't hurt during the surgery when you're asleep. After the surgery, pain medicines will help take care of the pain.

- Will I have a scar after surgery?
It's common to have a surgical scar, which can become lighter with time.

Rare Diseases

Doctors know how to give anesthesia and do surgery in ways that are safe for children. That's also true for many kids with rare diseases and unusual medical problems. You must talk to your team of doctors to participate in developing a safe plan for you. Don't be worried. You'll be in good hands!

Stethoscope

A stethoscope is a medical device that doctors and nurses use to listen to my heart as it beats and hear my lungs breathe. I'm thinking of using it to listen to my stomach growling today!

Fun fact: A stethoscope has 3 main parts: an earpiece, a tube, and a chest piece. The stethoscope can also be used to listen to my pulse and measure BP using a different machine.

Tubes

Notice all the tubes used during surgery.

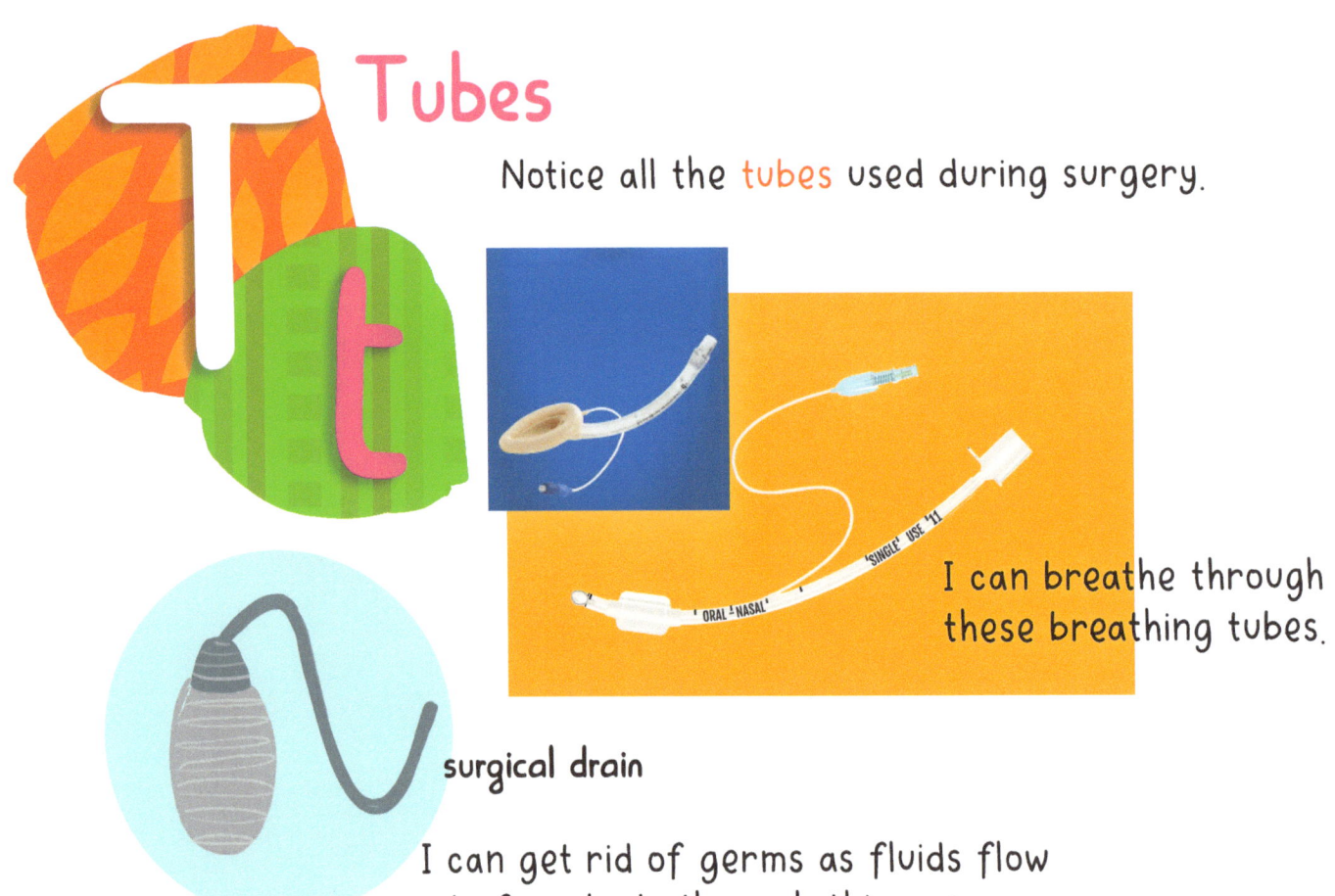

I can breathe through these breathing tubes.

surgical drain

I can get rid of germs as fluids flow out of my body through this one, called a surgical drain.

Fun fact: Let me tell you about another special tube! The Eustachian Tube is a narrow tube that connects the right and left middle ear to the back of your nose. When you're traveling in an airplane that is climbing or landing, the air pressure quickly changes. You can swallow or yawn at those times to open both eustachian tubes wider. Doing that allows each of your middle ears to get more air. it can relieve the pressure in your ears with that gentle pop!

Urine

I was told there would be no bathroom breaks during surgery! But I'm not worried. The nurse explained that they have a urine bag for that.
Did you know urine is a fancy name for pee?

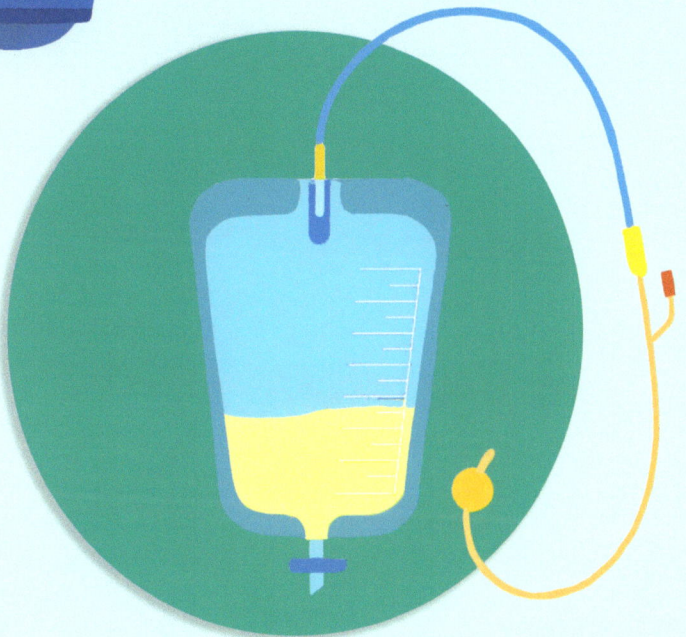

Fun fact: In one day, your body can produce between 750 and 1000 milliliters of urine (if you're a five-year-old child, for example). That amount of urine is equal to four or five cups of water!
So, you could pee between half a cup to two cups or more during surgery, depending on the length of time you're in the operating room.

Ventilator

While you sleep during surgery, a machine called a **ventilator** breathes for you. After you wake up from the anesthesia, you'll be able to breathe by yourself.

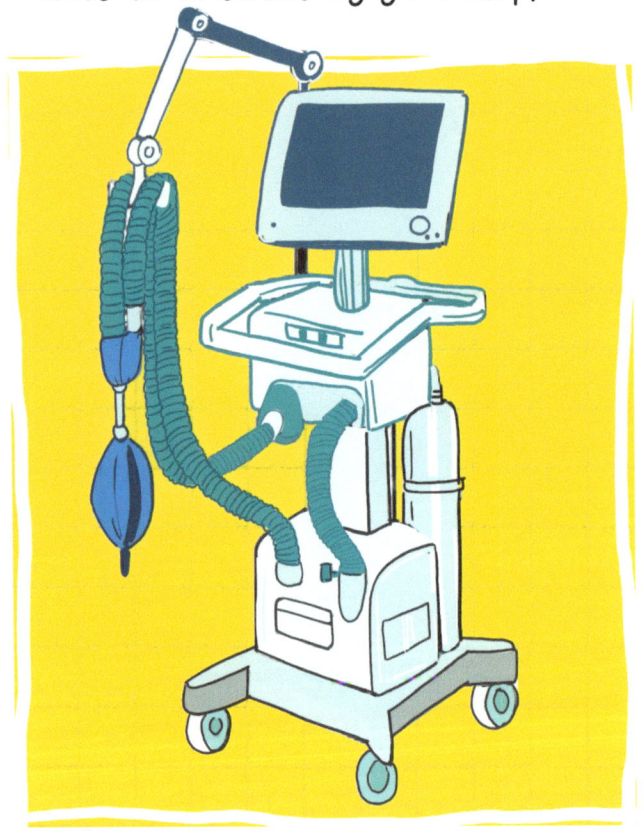

Fun fact: Ventilation is also a word used for the movement of air in the OR. These air changes (20-25 per hour) are needed to keep the temperature between 68°F (20°C) and 75°F (23.8°C). You can feel cold in the OR, but the team keeps you warm with blankets.

Waiting Room

The waiting room is a fun place for my family to wait while I'm having surgery. My buddy Cuddles is getting a good nap while waiting there for me.

Fun fact: The nurse will call and update the family members every hour so that they know all is well in the OR.

X-Ray

An X-ray is a special picture that shows my bones and lungs. The orthopedic surgeon will look at my X-ray to make sure the broken bone gets fixed the right way during surgery.

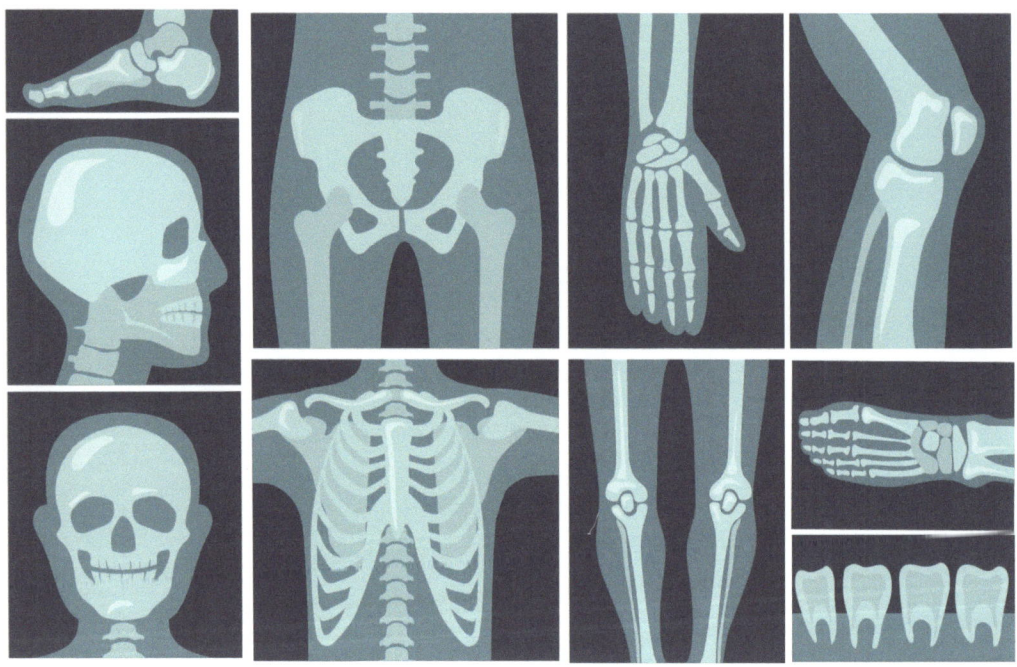

Fun fact: Besides seeing my bones, you can also see other things on the X-Ray. You can see my heart and my lungs; you can see if anything else is in my body that shouldn't be there! You can also see the X-Ray and find out if there any other problems going on.

Y y You

If you are the one having surgery, the most important person in the operating room is

YOU!
Go ahead and relax!
The awesome team of doctors and nurses are going to take very good care of you.

ZZZzzz...

I am in the operating room now, and the anesthesia is already making me sleepy.. I hope I have some sweet dreams. I am going to dream of amazing places, wonderlands with brave princesses who waltz and battle with ease and wear their crown with pride!

Fun fact: Anesthesia is like taking a little nap, when you wake up, everything will be all done!

Author: F.A. Khan

The author is an immigrant physician living in the US with her family. In her free time, she loves to read books, explore nature and travel. She enjoys writing stories about relationships, family connections and diversity. Her passion is to write about STEM topics for children in a fun interactive manner that encourages them to explore science with a new perspective.

Other books: My Superhero Mom, a children's book, and un-ed-ited, Healing Whispers, a poetry collection of her experiences as a physician, patient, caregiver and parent.

Author's note:

I was inspired to write this book and share my experiences after taking care of a little girl who came in with a broken arm for surgery. The little girl was scared and anxious, however, explaining the routine of surgery helped calm her down. She enjoyed being able to choose her own favorite bubblegum mask!

My daughter also had surgery when she was very young; I remember how scared she was. This book is a general outline on what to expect when you go for surgery. It will help you and your child be more prepared and understand what happens

Did you enjoy reading this book?

Let your teacher know to contact me for a school visit or book reading.

Email: fakhanauthor@gmail.com

https:///linktr.ee/ABCofmyFirstSurgery

@FAKhan_Author
www.GrandeReads.com

Illustrator : Bazma Ahmad

Bazma, is an illustrator with a passion for creating enchanting visuals. She has been drawing since childhood and has the pleasure of illustrating this amazing picture book by F.A.Khan . Children's books hold a special place in her heart, She is a published Illustrator, Graphic designer and an animator. She has done her Bachelors in Fine Arts from Jamia Millia Islamia and Masters in Animation from Delhi College of Arts, India.

Bazma's portfolio can be viewed at : www.bazmaahmad.com

K Answers below

knee	——	joint
kidney	——	urine
kyphosis	——	spine
ketamine	——	medicine
K - potassium	——	electrolyte
keloid	——	scar
keratin	——	protein
karyotype	——	DNA
keratitis	——	eyes

www.ingramcontent.com/pod-product-compliance
Ingram Content Group UK Ltd.
Pitfield, Milton Keynes, MK11 3LW, UK
UKHW060125240426
12049UKWH00013B/159